The World
and all that was
Made

The World and All That Was Made
by James Turner
Illustrated by Mariam Keinashvili

First printing: November 2021

ISBN: 978-1-946246-71-4

Please visit our website for other books and resources: ICR.org

Printed in the United States of America.

The World
and all that was
Made

by James Turner

INSTITUTE FOR
CREATION
RESEARCH

Dallas, TX
ICR.org

When we look at the world
and all that was made,
should there be any question
who gets the praise?

Jesus made the world
when it came to be,
and science confirms this
in all that we see.

Far out in space
we see blue stars
whose gases burn fast
like the fuel in our cars.

They can't last as long
as some scientists say.

Do you remember who made
the sun, moon, and stars
on the fourth day?

Mountains and canyons
are marvels to see,
and it didn't take millions of years
to bring them to be.

Noah's Flood made the canyons
as it drained off the land.
The force of its water
carved through rock, mud, and sand.

Remember the dinosaurs
who left fossils and tracks?
God gave them sharp teeth
to chomp plants as their snacks.

God said, "Job, look—
the behemoth I made along with you."
Dinosaurs are in the Bible;
did you know that it's true?

DIPLODOCUS

DIPLODOCUS

When you're out and about
and walking your path,
you'll find beautiful things
that are based upon math.

Like the spirals on a sunflower,
where God's order is displayed.
How could we see them
and not be amazed?

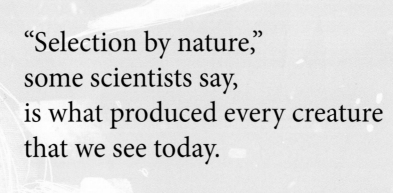

"Selection by nature,"
some scientists say,
is what produced every creature
that we see today.

But nature can't select anything;
it's God's great design

that keeps creatures' changes
within their own kind.

People are really something—
look at all we can do.
"Made in His image"
is certainly true!

We're like no other creature;
God set us apart.
And He's had a great plan for us
right from the start.

God has given us
so much more to explore.
Through His world and His Word,
we can learn even more.

All that Jesus has made,
all that Jesus has done,
should bring awe and wonder
to everyone.

Discover More Creation Facts About...

Blue Stars

Have you ever looked up in the sky on a dark night, away from city lights? The heavens twinkle with countless bright balls of burning gas—you know, stars. Blue stars are the hottest and burn brightest, which means they run out of fuel the fastest. And they're all over the universe! Blue stars can't last more than a million years. And no one has ever seen new stars forming to replace them. With so many blue stars still burning bright, how could the universe be billions of years old?

Mountains and Canyons

The global Flood changed our planet in big ways. Huge, moving slabs of crust and underground rock—called tectonic plates—broke the land into separate continents during the Flood. Where the plates slammed together, they pushed up mountains. Canyons formed when thick rock layers were deposited and then carved by a large amount of water from the end of Noah's Flood.

Dinosaurs

The word "dinosaur" was invented in 1841, long after the Bible was written. But in Job 40:15-18, the Bible describes a creature that sounds just like a long-necked dinosaur! Long-necks like *Brachiosaurus* ate plants—including grass. They had a unique hip design, and when they walked their tails swayed like a cedar tree swaying in the wind. When God told Job to look at the behemoth, he may have turned to see a real-life, in-the-flesh, stomping, crunching, munching dinosaur—a creature we only see as bare bones today.

Sunflowers

Our world is full of beautiful things, and it's by no accident! The spirals on a sunflower are based upon a math pattern called the Fibonacci sequence. And snowflakes form into unique shapes using a self-repeating pattern called a fractal. In Colossians 1:16-17, we see that God created all things, both visible and invisible—like math! So, we can give praise to God for the beauty and order that we see in all the things He has made.

Created Creatures

God made creatures with the ability to change themselves to fit their environment. The place where a creature lives does not cause it to change. Instead, the ability to change is designed into the creature! Genesis 1:25 tells us that God made creatures according to their kind. So, while we may see small changes within a creature kind over time, we will never see one creature turn into a completely different kind of creature.

The Human Body

Did you know that God receives glory when you use your body as He designed it to be used? As you swing a baseball bat, run a race, play piano, or kick a ball, you're showcasing God's incredible design. When you apply your creativity to art or invention, it points to the existence of an even greater Inventor and Creator—the Lord Jesus Christ—the One who made you!